SHARKS
AND OTHER HUNTERS OF THE DEEP

Written and illustrated by
Terry Riley

© Dean & Son Ltd., 1982
ISBN 0-603-00263-3

PRINTED IN **DEAN &** 52/54 Southwark St. **GREAT BRITAIN** **SON Ltd.** LONDON SE1 1UA
TRADE MARK

THE SHARKS

Of all the creatures in the sea, the one we most fear must be the shark. Certainly our fear and dread is justified with regard to some sharks, but not all sharks are man-eaters. Many are unjustly accused and, however wicked they may appear, are in fact harmless. Nevertheless we tend to think of all these superbly streamlined hunters as savage and deadly enemies.

Hundreds of millions of years ago, even before the mountain ranges of today had been forced up by violent movements of the Earth's continents, sharks swam in the seas. They belong to an incredibly long and ancient line of animals. By the time that our primitive ancestors began to evolve, all the kinds of sharks that we know today existed in their present forms. So our dread of the sea's most vicious hunters is an ancient fear that goes back to our very beginnings, and it is now that we are beginning to understand and learn about them.

From the various kinds of fossilized teeth that have been found, we have been able to trace the history of the sharks. Little else is preserved when a shark dies, for the shark's skeleton is made of cartilage, not of bone. Cartilage is like gristle, a strong but elastic substance, and unlike bone, it quickly degenerates when the animal dies.

Wrapped around its supple skeleton, the shark has massive banks of muscles running the entire length of its body, giving it immense power. A Blue Shark, for example, can dive faster than any submarine and swim at speeds of 50 kilometres (31 miles) an hour.

The vitality of sharks is amazing. They are always on the move, and even when terribly injured, sharks continue to fight. It has been reported that if disembowelled, they may even try to eat their own guts in their frenzy to find food.

Though the 250 or so kinds of sharks vary a great deal in size, from a few centimetres or inches to more than 15 metres (50 feet), they share many typical features. A shark's teeth are not socketed in the jaw, as ours are. They keep on growing throughout the shark's life and move forward in rows towards the outside edge of the mouth. As old ones fall out, the rows of new teeth move forward, inserting fresh wickedly-sharp barbs in their place.

Prey must be detected if this regiment of teeth is to be put to use. The sense of smell is the prime guide in this respect, a shark being capable of detecting odours at a distance of more than 2.5 kilometres (1½ miles).

The 'nostrils' of a shark are not used in breathing, for they are the passages that lead to remarkably sensitive smell detectors. When a kill is made and blood stains the water, the area soon abounds with more frenzied hunters, swiftly gliding in to the kill as if from nowhere at the merest whiff of blood.

Pleuracanthus, a small freshwater shark, hunted for fish in the lakes of the Carboniferous Period 300 million years ago.

After their sense of smell, sharks use their hearing to find prey, and it is accompanied by a sense of 'touch'. This is the shark's ability to feel vibrations made in the water by moving objects, and this sensitivity can guide the shark to within striking distance of possible prey. At this point, sight becomes useful and the eyes of some deep-water varieties have special cells which intensify light. This is a most useful asset in the dim light that prevails in the vast regions of the deep.

Sharks are constantly on the move because, unlike fish, they do not possess air bladders to keep them afloat. If it stops swimming, a shark begins to sink—which could mean death for many varieties. Unlike most fish, the gills of some sharks are equipped with weak muscles, and cannot move quickly enough or open wide enough to allow a large flow of water to pass over them if the shark ceases to move forward. A constant flow of water over and through the gills is necessary for these organs to extract oxygen from the water, and enable the shark to breathe. If the flow ceases, then the shark suffocates.

Apart from the gigantic Whale Shark, the largest of all fish, sharks have an obvious common feature: their streamlined form. This shape is perfect for a hunter of the seas, giving a speed and manoeuvrability almost unmatched in the oceans. It is a form so well designed that it has not needed to be altered for millions and millions of years, a triumph of evolution.

Several sharks readily attack people if the opportunity presents itself, but the main diet of all except the largest two varieties is fish. The 12-metre (40 feet) long Basking Shark, and the even larger Whale Shark, are both plankton feeders.

Sharks eat man but man also eats shark, particularly the small Dogfish. Dogfish is an excellent fish, having more protein and energy value than Salmon, Lobster, eggs or milk. Apart from its value as food, fishermen once sought this little shark for its skin. This is rough yet fine and strong, and it was used to polish wood and even metals.

The Common Spotted Dogfish is the most plentiful shark of the North Sea area.

The tropical waters of the world hold many more sharks than the colder seas of the north. However, annual migrations of many species, and in particular those of the Blue Shark, bring thousands of these hunters to waters around the British Isles.

In early summer, Blue Sharks leave the warmer waters of the south Atlantic Ocean and travel north. They are a common sight in the sea off Cornwall from the middle of June onwards. If the warm waters of the Gulf Stream are flowing strongly, then the sharks will ride farther on the current to Scotland and beyond, some ending up as far north as Norway.

Strangely, almost all the Blue Sharks which visit the north-east Atlantic have been found to be females, many of them pregnant. On the north-west (the American) side of the Atlantic, nearly all the migrating Blue Sharks are males.

The Blue Shark is known to be a man-eater, but this is only because it is a species that will take advantage of any situation offering the chance of a meal. It does not consider people as some sort of delicacy, and will eat anything. The stomachs of some Blue Sharks have been opened for inspection, revealing many items which must have fallen or have been thrown overboard from ships. The contents of one dead Blue Shark, for example, contained such odd things as bottles, two sheep heads, an old shoe, the complete hindquarters of a pig, and, most surprising of all, the entire body of a dog complete with its collar and lead!

As well as the Blue Shark, many other sharks are often seen in the seas around Britain. The Porbeagle Shark is in fact a resident that breeds in the cool waters around our coasts. Like the Blue Shark, the female Porbeagle Shark gives birth to live young which are about 50 centimetres ($1\frac{1}{2}$ feet) long at birth. The number of young sharks born depends upon the size of the mother, but usually varies from one to four.

The Blue Shark and the Porbeagle
(bottom) both inhabit British waters.

The Mako Shark is a summer visitor to Britain, and is a fish which is popular with people who fish for sharks as sport. This is because, unlike a Porbeagle, a Mako will fight if hooked. Leaping and struggling to avoid capture, its almost 200-kilogram (440 lbs) bulk sometimes shoots high out of the water in a frenzy to escape.

Like the Mako, another shark leaves the deep waters of the ocean to enter our seas in summer. This is the peculiar Thresher Shark. A slim body ending in an enormously long tail makes the uncommon Thresher Shark unmistakable in appearance. Growing to some 6 metres (20 feet) long and weighing almost 350 kilograms (770 lbs), half its length is taken up by a huge sickle-shaped tail used to thrash the water while circling a shoal of fish. This action seems to force the fish into a tight group, and the shark then charges at them and gulps them down.

Largest of all the regular migrants to British Seas is the huge but harmless Basking Shark. This 11-metre (36 feet) giant feeds only on plankton and so has no large sharp teeth. Its name comes from the fact that it is often seen basking at the surface, when its back fin and snout are visible above the water. In the past, this habit made Basking Sharks easy prey and they were harpooned like whales, and their livers cut out to make oil.

Basking Sharks swim with their mouths opened like huge caverns, so that the tiny plankton animals on which they feed are swept in. Special bristles comb the enormous volume of sea water passing through, capturing the plankton which is then swallowed.

Plankton consists of various kinds of fish eggs, tiny crabs, shrimps and suchlike, depending on the variety of sea life in any particular place. While small in size, plankton animals are not insignificant in nature, for they are the food source of many creatures apart from the Basking Shark. Most famous of these is the very largest animal on Earth, the Blue Whale.

The fish-eating Thresher has an enormously long tail fin.

SHARKS IN SOUTHERN WATERS

The warmer oceans of the world are home to a host of different sharks. Bathers from the shores of the mid-Atlantic states of America to the sandy beaches of southern Australia can never swim entirely without risk of a shark attack. Even people that bathe in rivers there run the risk of being killed or injured by a shark.

Unlike most marine fish, sharks can readily adapt to life in fresh water. However, they often find themselves short of food in the less abundant larder of a river. Consequently, the sharks will turn from chasing the few fast fishes there to the slow and easy target of a human being, should one ever present itself. In Iran, during an eight year period, more than a dozen people died in a total of 27 shark attacks along the Karun River.

It is thought that sharks do not enter rivers primarily to feed but to rid themselves of parasites, which loose their grip on their host when immersed in fresh water. Not only tropical rivers receive these visits however, for sharks have also been seen as far as 50 kilometres (31 miles) up the Delaware River in North America. They have also been spotted in the murky canals of Venice!

The appetite of a shark is prodigal, and this seemingly insatiable hunter spends its whole life in a constant search for ways of easing its terrible hunger. Consequently, a shark is an efficient cleaner of the oceans as well as a voracious predator. The mouth, being situated on the underside of its head, allows the shark to scavenge off the sea bed if killing has not provided it with enough to eat.

Some sharks can rest on the sea bottom, should the urge to eat be momentarily satisfied. Tiger Sharks, and a few other kinds, have been observed resting with their bellies on the sea bed. These varieties have sufficient muscle power to pump water slowly through their gills, supplying the required oxygen to their bodies. But sharks are more often occupied in a constant slow cruise as they search the sea—a cruise that may take them on journeys of some 60,000 kilometres (37,000 miles) in a year.

A Hawaiian Monk Seal being attacked by Grey-and-White Tipped Reef Sharks.

A Sand Shark with its company of attendants: Pilot Fish and a hitchhiking Remora.

Most sharks are accompanied during their travels by Pilot Fish, and many of these wolves of the sea also carry passengers as they roam the vast waters of the world. Pilot Fish are the shark's constant companions; they swim just in front of their protector's wicked jaws and feed on the leavings of its kills. Just why the shark never eats these striped opportunists is not known. It is an odd and mysterious partnership in the struggle for existence.

The shark's non-paying passengers are called Remoras. These fish attach themselves to the shark's body by sucker discs on top of their heads, and they too probably feed on scraps left by their host. Remoras also attach themselves to other large fish, turtles, whales and even boats, as they hitchhike around the oceans. But should a host not be available for free transport, the Remora is quite capable of doing its own swimming.

The largest family of sharks has members which inhabit all the shallow parts of tropical and temperate oceans. Sand Sharks belong to this group, and they are common scavengers. Like all their tribe, they must be considered potentially dangerous and are suspected of being responsible for many attacks upon bathers, especially in Australian waters, where 3-metre (10-feet) long specimens are common. The eastern coast of Australia is the most dangerous place to bathe in the world, as more shark attacks occur there than anywhere else. Other trouble spots are South Africa and parts of America. Why these places should have more inshore incidents than others is still not fully understood.

GOOD BAD AND UGLY

Most peculiar in appearance of all the sharks is the 5-metre (16-feet) long Hammerhead Shark. This hunter differs from all other sharks in having a most strange head. Its eyes are located on the end of two outward projecting growths, which give the fish its odd name. While individual in design, the Hammerhead Shark follows the same life style as its more conventional cousins. It feeds on fish and has a liking for Sting Rays, apparently able to disregard their poisonous barbed tails. It also considers people with the same apparent lack of fear, for it is one of the varieties held responsible for attacks upon swimmers.

However, the fiercest and most dangerous of all man-eaters is the Great White Shark, which can exceed 7 metres (23 feet) in length. It is very swift even though it is so big, for large specimens may weigh as much as one tonne.

The Great White Shark, or White Pointer as it is sometimes called, has a huge mouth containing dozens of teeth only 7 centimetres (2½ inches) long. Though short, these saw-like triangles of death have even bitten great chunks out of wooden boats, for fishing vessels are considered worthy of the White Pointer's attention. When the deadly fish moves close inshore, almost anything that moves is attacked. Fish, marine turtles, seals, other sharks and man all fall foul of this massive predator. When one huge specimen was cut open, an entire horse was revealed! Even an elephant wading in the surf of a Kenyan beach was once attacked by a Great White Shark.

The harmless Nurse Shark and the deadly Hammerhead both inhabit warm shallow waters.

Some waters are often described as being 'shark infested', but none more so than the places where Sand Tigers are found. Sand Tigers, or Common Sand Sharks, often hunt in packs of a hundred or more and herd shoals of fish towards shallow water. In Atlantic waters, they hunt the Bluefish. When these wolves of the sea have driven them into a corner from which they cannot escape, they launch their attack.

Largest of all the sharks in the world, and indeed of all the fishes, are the Whale Sharks. These monstrous fish can grow to almost 20 metres (66 feet) long and weigh several tonnes. Like Basking Sharks, these whale-like creatures feed upon plankton. They are so docile that they allow divers to approach them, and even tolerate the human intruders riding them by holding onto their gigantic back fins. These peaceful giants of the deep are hunted in some places, for the liver of a Whale Shark may contain more than 600 litres (132 gallons) of oil.

The sluggish monster does not possess the agility and speed characteristic of sharks, nor does it constantly break the surface in order to breathe as true whales do. This spotted brown colossus usually drifts slowly along near the surface, and has often been rammed by ships.

Many sharks give birth to live young, but the Whale Shark lays eggs. The huge cases containing the eggs are deposited in the deep waters of the tropical Atlantic, Indian and Pacific oceans.

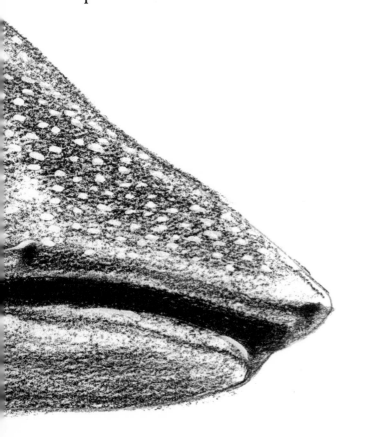

A diver may approach the massive spotted Whale Shark for the plankton eater is a docile creature.

Even though most sharks are highly dangerous predators and do not flinch from attacking almost anything that enters their domain, they do not always have things all their own way. They may be attacked by other sharks, and may have to face assaults by swordfish. Even the normally peaceful dolphins have sometimes been known to beat a shark to death by repeatedly charging it head-on, then ramming into it at high speed. However, the shark's main enemy is man. Many people make a sport of killing sharks, and around resorts, sharks are exterminated to protect bathers. Many are killed to provide us with food, including Dogfish, Tope and the famous Soupfin Shark, provider of sharksfin soup (a delicacy rich in vitamin A).

So the hunter is more often hunted by man than the other way round. However, no one would deny which of the two species seems better equipped by nature to fulfil a hunter's role. No creatures have such a savage reputation as do sharks. In ten years, one may get through some 24,000 teeth, powered by muscles that can exert a biting force capable of cutting most opponents in half with one mighty bite. This is a thought we should have constantly in mind whenever we enter the sea, the kingdom of the most deadly of hunters—the shark.

The savage mouth of the Great White Shark.

THE SPERM WHALE

The oceans contain many other fearsome hunters as well as sharks, some of them gigantic creatures. But we can never witness the most awe-inspiring of nature's battles, for it takes place in the constant midnight of the ocean deeps. The opponents are both huge and powerful, each some 15 metres (50 feet) long and capable of inflicting terrible wounds. They are the mighty Sperm Whale and the Giant Squid.

A Sperm Whale dives some 650 metres (over 2000 feet) to enter the realm of the Giant Squid. Even though its opponent can defend itself with vigour, the mightiest of hunting whales searches it out in the inky blackness of the silent deep, for each squid promises the whale a one tonne meal. The Sperm Whale has to contend with the tentacled arms of its prey, which bear hundreds of large suction discs able to hold tight and bite deeply into the whale's dark hide. Many captured Sperm Whales show huge circular scars, indicating that the Giant Squid could have arms more than 18 metres (60 feet) long! These monsters have yet to be seen alive by man, but the Sperm Whale knows them well.

After a deep dive, the Sperm Whale heads for the surface to breathe, blowing a fountain of spray into the air. The arching spout often betrays the whale's presence to a predator that it has no chance of beating—man. When the Sperm Whale was hunted in wooden whaling boats rowed by half-a-dozen men with a harpooner in the bow, it often fought back and won. Its massive teeth and powerful tail proved as useful against man as they did against the Giant Squid. Today, exploding harpoons fired from high-powered boats give the Sperm Whale no chance. Each year brings the species closer to extinction.

Sperm Whales roam the oceans in family groups usually led by an old 'bull' whale. He is accompanied by a number of females ('cows') and youngsters, whom he protects until summer approaches. Then he leaves and migrates to the colder seas, there to meet up with other males. They feed on fish, squid, even sharks, and then return to their families, often a tonne heavier after the summer's hunting.

In the days when there were no man-made alternatives to the products extracted from whales, such as oil, hunting them had some justification. Now it has none. Science has invented products that are good substitutes for those made from the bodies of dead whales, and so man can and should stop killing Sperm Whales and other whales, before the seas are empty of the mightiest creations of nature.

THE KILLER WHALE

One of the most intelligent of all marine mammals is the Orca or Killer Whale. In recent years, this hunter has been kept in captivity, where it is a non-aggressive, sociable creature. In the environment of the aquarium, the Killer Whale has never attacked its keepers, and it obviously enjoys contact with people.

However, in the wild, Killer Whales hunt in packs and attack animals as large as the plankton-eating baleen whales, which reach 28 metres (92 feet) in length. Hunting in groups or alone, this black-and-white cousin of the dolphins is a feared and crafty predator. Seals, squid, dolphins and, in the Antarctic, penguins all fall prey to the skilful killer.

Should a seal or penguin hear the powerful, regular beat that signals the approach of a school of Killer Whales, then they may seek safety on a handy ice floe. But escape is not so easy. Their hunter is equipped with an echo-sounding device that informs it of any movement or obstacle in the surrounding waters. It is able to detect that its prey is seeking refuge on the drifting sea ice. In a rush of water, the Orca rams the ice floe, tilting or shattering it and throwing the terrified prey into the sea, where it cannot flee the massive jaws. Killers they may be, but never for 'sport'. Orcas kill to eat.

Killer Whales also use their ability to make and detect sounds to keep in touch with others, as we do. They have a large vocabulary of sounds, which to us sound like grunts, squeaks and clicks. The meaning of this whale language is not yet totally understood, though many scientists are making intensive studies of it.

The female uses clicking sounds to reassure her calf, as she circles protectively around it. She feeds the young whale for a year before it becomes independent of its mother, and then it joins a pack or school of whales. It grows into one of the most inquisitive, sensitive and intelligent of mammals. Unlike the two-legged mammal that hunts for sport, the Orca kills only to survive, in an environment that has supported its kind for 40 million years.

THE MORAY EEL

The sea holds many hunting animals, far more than those that can be seen at the surface, such as sharks. A black triangular fin cutting through the blue sea is a clear and unmistakable warning that a hunter is on the prowl. Beneath the surface, skulking within the dark crevices of coral reefs and rock formations or inside the silent shells of sunken ships, other predators hide and await unwary or inquisitive prey.

One of the most dangerous of these stealthy killers that live in the dark corners of the oceans is the Moray Eel. Found in all tropical and temperate seas, there are many variations in the eel's colour but none in temperament. All Morays are extremely dangerous and unpredictable creatures.

As the Moray Eel quietly surveys its surroundings, only the regular gulping movement of its mouth may betray its presence. This action is necessary to take water into the gill chambers for breathing. It displays the eel's teeth, a regiment of needlesharp weapons feared by divers, and rightly so. If a skin diver allows an arm or leg to enter an apparently empty cavity in a reef, it could be grasped by the curved teeth of a resident Moray, and the eel would hang on grimly. A fully-grown Moray Eel may be almost 2 metres (6½ feet) long, and with its lithe but muscular body anchored around the rock or coral, the captured diver would have to rip himself free, for the tenacious eel would never simply let go.

The Atlantic variety of this eel is called the Green Moray. Its skin is actually blue, but it is covered in a yellow slime which makes it look green.

Many colourful varieties exist in more tropical waters, and the addition of spots and bars of contrasting shades make these already fearsome creatures look even more bizarre and awesome. Morays feed on fish, and usually only come out of hiding to strike down their prey at night.

Animals such as the Moray Eel, which steals into hiding places to kill, or sharks which destroy with demonic fury in a seemingly uncontrollable rage, are obviously fixed in our minds as repulsive creatures, fit only for extermination. But once we look at those hunters with the aim of understanding their place in the world, then fear may be replaced with respect. All such animals play a vital role in the balance of nature, the interaction of predators and prey essential to the maintenance of all life on Earth.